One Sentence Storybooks

BIBLE

The Sun and the Moon

WRITTEN BY **Nancy I. Sanders** ILLUSTRATED BY **Hannah Wood**

This book is dedicated to Ryan Lawrence Sanders

One Sentence Storybooks: *The Sun and the Moon* text copyright © 2015 Nancy I. Sanders. All rights reserved. ·
Illustrations copyright © 2015 Hannah Wood. All rights reserved. · *Focus on the Family* and the accompanying logo
and design are federally registered trademarks of Focus on the Family, 8605 Explorer Drive, Colorado Springs, CO
80920. · *TYNDALE* is a registered trademark of Tyndale House Publishers, Inc. The Tyndale Kids logo is a trademark
of Tyndale House Publishers, Inc. · No part of this publication may be reproduced, stored in a retrieval system, or
transmitted in any form or by any means—electronic, mechanical, photocopy, recording, or otherwise—without prior
written permission of Focus on the Family. · Scripture taken from the Holy Bible, *New International Reader's Version*,®
NIrV® Copyright © 1995, 1996, 1998 by Biblica, Inc.® Used by permission of Zondervan. All rights reserved worldwide.
www.zondervan.com. · Cover design by Stephen Vosloo · The author is represented by HERMAN AGENCY, Ronnie@
HermanAgencyInc.com (www.HermanAgencyInc.com).
For manufacturing information regarding this product, please call 1-800-323-9400.
Printed in China
21 20 19 18 17 16 15   7 6 5 4 3 2 1

God's hand

God's hand

made the sun

God's hand
made the sun
and the moon

God's hand
made the sun
and the moon
and the earth.

hand

sun

moon

earth

One Truth to Learn

The Bible says that God spoke and the world was created.

One Verse to Say

Memorize this verse with your child:

"Didn't my powerful hand make everything? That is how all things were created," *announces the Lord.* — Isaiah 66:2

One Prayer to Pray

Thank You, Jesus, for making the whole wide world. Thank You for making me. In Your name, amen.

Look Back in the Book

Point to something **white**.

Find two circles.

Read the word that starts with the

same sound as 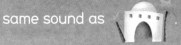. *Answer: hand*

For more faith-building activities to do with
your child, visit *onesentencestorybooks.com*.

One Sentence Storybooks

BIBLE FAVORITES

Two Mice and the Ark

WRITTEN BY **Nancy I. Sanders** ILLUSTRATED BY **Hannah Wood**

This book is dedicated to Deanna Overstreet

For manufacturing information regarding this product, please call 1-800-323-9400.
Printed in China
21 20 19 18 17 16 15   7 6 5 4 3 2 1

Two mice

Two mice

and two cats

Two mice

and two cats

and two dogs

Two mice

and two cats

and two dogs

ran into the ark.

 mice

 cats

 dogs

 ark

One Truth to Learn

Sin is anything bad someone thinks, says, or does. God sent a flood to get rid of sin on the earth. But He used an ark to save Noah, his family, and the animals.

One Verse to Say

Memorize this verse with your child:

> [Jesus said,] "I didn't come to judge the world. I came to save it." — John 12:47

One Prayer to Pray

Thank You, God, that You forgive us for our sins when we tell You we're sorry. In Jesus' name, amen.

Look Back in the Book

Point to something **pink**.

Count the spots on the giraffes.

Read the word that starts with

the same sound as . *Answer: mice.*

For more faith-building activities to do with
your child, visit *onesentencestorybooks.com*.

One Sentence Storybooks

B I B L E   F A V O R I T E S

Moses and the Bush

WRITTEN BY **Nancy I. Sanders** ILLUSTRATED BY **Hannah Wood**

This book is dedicated to Tom Overstreet

One Sentence Storybooks: *Moses and the Bush* text copyright © 2015 Nancy I. Sanders. All rights reserved. · Illustrations copyright © 2015 Hannah Wood. All rights reserved. · *Focus on the Family* and the accompanying logo and design are federally registered trademarks of Focus on the Family, 8605 Explorer Drive, Colorado Springs, CO 80920. · TYNDALE is a registered trademark of Tyndale House Publishers, Inc. The Tyndale Kids logo is a trademark of Tyndale House Publishers, Inc. · No part of this publication may be reproduced, stored in a retrieval system, or transmitted in any form or by any means—electronic, mechanical, photocopy, recording, or otherwise—without prior written permission of Focus on the Family. · Scripture taken from the Holy Bible, *New International Reader's Version,*® NIrV® Copyright © 1995, 1996, 1998 by Biblica, Inc.® Used by permission of Zondervan. All rights reserved worldwide. www.zondervan.com. · Cover design by Stephen Vosloo. · The author is represented by HERMAN AGENCY, Ronnie@HermanAgencyInc.com (www.HermanAgencyInc.com).

For manufacturing information regarding this product, please call 1-800-323-9400.

Printed in China

21 20 19 18 17 16 15   7 6 5 4 3 2 1

Moses

Moses

saw a bush

Moses

saw a bush

that was on fire

Moses

saw a bush

that was on fire

and took off his shoes.

Moses

bush

fire

shoes

One Truth to Learn

God spoke to Moses from inside the burning bush. God gave Moses an important job to do.

One Verse to Say

Memorize this verse with your child:

I can do everything by the power of [Jesus] Christ. He gives me strength. — Philippians 4:13

One Prayer to Pray

Dear God, please use me to do something important for You. In Jesus' name, amen.

Look Back in the Book

Point to something *orange*.

Count all the yellow stripes in Moses' hat.

Read the word that starts with the

same sound as . *Answer: bush*

For more faith-building activities to do with your child, visit *onesentencestorybooks.com*.

One Sentence Storybooks
BIBLE FAVORITES

David and the Giant

WRITTEN BY **Nancy I. Sanders** ILLUSTRATED BY **Hannah Wood**

This book is dedicated to Ben Sanders

For manufacturing information regarding this product, please call 1-800-323-9400.
Printed in China
21 20 19 18 17   16   15   7 6 5 4 3 2 1

David

David

hit the lion

David

hit the lion

and the bear

David

hit the lion

and the bear

and the giant.

 David

 lion

 bear

 giant

One Truth to Learn

David knew God was the one who saved him from the lion, the bear, and the giant.

One Verse to Say

Memorize this verse with your child:

The LORD your God is with you. He is mighty enough to save you. — Zephaniah 3:17

One Prayer to Pray

Dear God, You are mighty! I trust You will save me from evil, and I ask You to calm all my worries and fears. In Jesus' name, amen.

Look Back in the Book

Point to something **purple**.

Count all the claws on the bear's paws.

Read the word that starts with the

same sound as *Answer: giant*

For more faith-building activities to do with
your child, visit *onesentencestorybooks.com*.

One Sentence Storybooks
BIBLE FAVORITES

The City Wall

WRITTEN BY **Nancy I. Sanders** *ILLUSTRATED BY* **Hannah Wood**

This book is dedicated to Stuart Dautrich

For manufacturing information regarding this product, please call 1-800-323-9400.
Printed in China
21 20 19 18 17 16 15   7 6 5 4 3 2 1

The people

The people
in the city

The people

in the city

picked up rocks

The people
in the city
picked up rocks
to make the wall.

people

 city

 rocks

 wall

One Truth to Learn

Nehemiah prayed to God for protection. Then he got all the people to help rebuild the city wall.

One Verse to Say

Memorize this verse with your child:

The prayer of a godly person is powerful. It makes things happen. — James 5:16

One Prayer to Pray

Please protect the people in my life and give them strength, God. In Jesus' name, amen.

Look Back in the Book

Point to something blue.

Count the points on each tree.

Read the word that starts with the

same sound as   . *Answer: wall*

One Sentence Storybooks

BIBLE FAVORITES

The Star and the Kings

WRITTEN BY **Nancy I. Sanders** ILLUSTRATED BY **Hannah Wood**

This book is dedicated to Emma Dautrich

For manufacturing information regarding this product, please call 1-800-323-9400.
Printed in China
21 20 19 18 17 16 15   7 6 5 4 3 2 1

The star

The star

in the sky

The star

in the sky

led the kings

The star

in the sky

led the kings

to baby Jesus.

star

 sky

 kings

 baby Jesus

One Truth to Learn

The kings worshiped baby Jesus when they found Him.

One Verse to Say

Memorize this verse with your child:

Come, let us bow down and worship him. Let us fall on our knees in front of the Lord our Maker. He is our God. — Psalm 95:6-7

One Prayer to Pray

Dear Jesus, I worship You today. You are the King of kings, and I praise Your holy name. Amen.

Look Back in the Book

Point to something gold.

Find four dots on a crown.

Read the words that start with the same sound as . *Answer: baby Jesus*

For more faith-building activities to do with your child, visit *onesentencestorybooks.com*.

One Sentence Storybooks
BIBLE FAVORITES

Jesus on the Water

WRITTEN BY **Nancy I. Sanders** ILLUSTRATED BY **Hannah Wood**

This book is dedicated to Joy Dautrich

For manufacturing information regarding this product, please call 1-800-323-9400.
Printed in China
21 20 19 18 17 16 15   7 6 5 4 3 2 1

The men

The men
in the boat

The men

in the boat

saw Jesus

The men
in the boat
saw Jesus
walk on water.

 men

 boat

 Jesus

 water

One Truth to Learn

The disciples' faith grew after they saw Jesus walk on water. Jesus really is the Son of God.

One Verse to Say

Memorize this verse with your child:

> *Those in the boat worshiped Jesus.*
> *They said, "You really are the Son of God!"*
> — Matthew 14:33

One Prayer to Pray

Dear God, please help my faith grow stronger every day. In Jesus' name, amen.

Look Back in the Book

Point to something green.

Find something with stripes.

Read the word that starts with

the same sound as . *Answer: men*

One Sentence Storybooks
BIBLE FAVORITES

The Good Shepherd

WRITTEN BY Nancy I. Sanders ILLUSTRATED BY Hannah Wood

This book is dedicated to Ryan's uncles

One Sentence Storybooks: *The Good Shepherd* text copyright © 2015 Nancy I. Sanders. All rights reserved. · Illustrations copyright © 2015 Hannah Wood. All rights reserved. · *Focus on the Family* and the accompanying logo and design are federally registered trademarks of Focus on the Family, 8605 Explorer Drive, Colorado Springs, CO 80920. · *TYNDALE* is a registered trademark of Tyndale House Publishers, Inc. The Tyndale Kids logo is a trademark of Tyndale House Publishers, Inc. · No part of this publication may be reproduced, stored in a retrieval system, or transmitted in any form or by any means—electronic, mechanical, photocopy, recording, or otherwise—without prior written permission of Focus on the Family. · Scripture taken from the Holy Bible, *New International Reader's Version,*® *NIrV*® Copyright © 1995, 1996, 1998 by Biblica, Inc.® Used by permission of Zondervan. All rights reserved worldwide. www.zondervan.com. · Cover design by Stephen Vosloo. · The author is represented by HERMAN AGENCY, Ronnie@HermanAgencyInc.com (www.HermanAgencyInc.com).

For manufacturing information regarding this product, please call 1-800-323-9400.

Printed in China

21 20 19 18 17 16 15   7 6 5 4 3 2 1

The Good Shepherd

The Good Shepherd

with the sheep

The Good Shepherd

with the sheep

got his lost lamb

The Good Shepherd
with the sheep
got his lost lamb
and had joy.

Good Shepherd

sheep

lamb

joy

One Truth to Learn

The angels in heaven rejoice each time a child trusts in Jesus to save him or her.

One Verse to Say

Memorize this verse with your child:

> [Jesus said,] "I am the good shepherd. The good shepherd gives his life for the sheep."
> — John 10:11

One Prayer to Pray

Dear God, thank You for loving me and being my Good Shepherd. In Jesus' name, amen.

Look Back in the Book

Point to something **red**.

Count the legs of all the sheep.

Read the word that starts with the same sound as . *Answer: lamb*

For more faith-building activities to do with your child, visit *onesentencestorybooks.com*.

One Sentence Storybooks
B I B L E   F A V O R I T E S

The Sad Son

WRITTEN BY **Nancy I. Sanders** ILLUSTRATED BY **Hannah Wood**

This book is dedicated to Ryan's aunts

For manufacturing information regarding this product, please call 1-800-323-9400.
Printed in China
21 20 19 18 17 16 15   7 6 5 4 3 2 1

The sad son

The sad son

came back home

The sad son
came back home
to his dad

The sad son
came back home
to his dad
for a hug.

son

home

dad

hug

One Truth to Learn

God is our loving Father. God always loves us and will always forgive us.

One Verse to Say

Memorize this verse with your child:

How great is the love the Father has given us so freely! Now we can be called children of God. — 1 John 3:1

One Prayer to Pray

Dear God, I'm glad You are my Father and that You love me. I love You too. In Jesus' name, amen.

Look Back in the Book

Point to something **brown**.

Find something square.

Read the word that starts with the same sound as . *Answer: dad*

For more faith-building activities to do with your child, visit *onesentencestorybooks.com*.

One Sentence Storybooks
BIBLE FAVORITES

The Angel and the Cave

WRITTEN BY **Nancy I. Sanders** ILLUSTRATED BY **Hannah Wood**

This book is dedicated to Christina Sanders

One Sentence Storybooks: *The Angel and the Cave* text copyright © 2015 Nancy I. Sanders. All rights reserved. · Illustrations copyright © 2015 Hannah Wood. All rights reserved. · *Focus on the Family* and the accompanying logo and design are federally registered trademarks of Focus on the Family, 8605 Explorer Drive, Colorado Springs, CO 80920. · TYNDALE is a registered trademark of Tyndale House Publishers, Inc. The Tyndale Kids logo is a trademark of Tyndale House Publishers, Inc. · No part of this publication may be reproduced, stored in a retrieval system, or transmitted in any form or by any means—electronic, mechanical, photocopy, recording, or otherwise—without prior written permission of Focus on the Family. · Scripture taken from the Holy Bible, *New International Reader's Version,*® NIrV® Copyright © 1995, 1996, 1998 by Biblica, Inc.® Used by permission of Zondervan. All rights reserved worldwide. www.zondervan.com. · Cover design by Stephen Vosloo. · The author is represented by HERMAN AGENCY, Ronnie@HermanAgencyInc.com (www.HermanAgencyInc.com).

For manufacturing information regarding this product, please call 1-800-323-9400.

Printed in China

21 20 19 18 17 16 15   7 6 5 4 3 2 1

The angel

The angel
on the hill

The angel

on the hill

pushed the stone

The angel

on the hill

pushed the stone

from the cave.

angel

hill

stone

cave

One Truth to Learn

Jesus died on the cross and was buried in a cave-like tomb. The tomb was sealed shut with a large stone. But when the angel rolled the stone away, the tomb was empty. Jesus is alive!

One Verse to Say

Memorize this verse with your child:

> *[Jesus] was buried. He was raised from the dead on the third day, just as [the Bible] said he would be.* — 1 Corinthians 15:4

One Prayer to Pray

I praise You, God, for the empty tomb. In Jesus' name, amen.

Look Back in the Book

Point to something yellow.

Find something round.

Read the word that starts with the same sound as .   *Answer: cave*

For more faith-building activities to do with your child, visit *onesentencestorybooks.com*.